fondue

simple and delicious easy-to-make recipes

Lorraine Turner

Marks and Spencer p.l.c.
Baker Street, London, W1U 8EP

www.marksandspencer.com

ISBN: 1-84273-977-8

Printed in China

Produced by the Bridgewater Book Company Ltd.

Photographer Calvey Taylor-Haw

Home Economist Ruth Pollock

NOTES FOR THE READER

- This book uses both metric and imperial measurements. Follow the same units of measurement throughout; do not mix metric and imperial.

- All spoon measurements are level: teaspoons are assumed to be 5 ml, and tablespoons are assumed to be 15 ml.

- Unless otherwise stated, milk is assumed to be full fat, eggs and individual vegetables such as potatoes are medium and pepper is freshly ground black pepper.

- Recipes using raw or very lightly cooked eggs should be avoided by infants, the elderly, pregnant women, convalescents and anyone suffering from an illness.

- Optional ingredients, variations or serving suggestions have not been included in the calculations. The times given are an approximate guide only. Preparation times differ according to the techniques used by different people and the cooking times may also vary from those given.

contents

introduction

Fondues are excellent for entertaining: who can resist spearing tempting morsels of food on to fondue forks and dipping them into a simmering pot of something delicious at the dinner table?

The word 'fondue' comes from the French word *fondre*, which means 'melt'. The classic melted cheese fondue originated in Switzerland, and many exciting variations have since emerged. Stock fondues provide a healthy low-fat alternative, where diners immerse pieces of food into a pot of simmering stock and cook them to their taste. Oil-based fondues are higher in fat, but equally delicious. Fondues also make wonderful desserts. You will find a good selection of all these in this book.

Earthenware fondue pots are often used for cheese fondues. However, they will not withstand the higher cooking temperatures needed for stock- or oil-based fondues, so choose instead a pot made from stainless steel or enamelled cast iron. Place the pot securely over the burner: it should never be top heavy. Remember also, when you lift out your cooked food from the pot, to transfer it to your plate or to a different fork before eating. This courteous practice protects against burnt mouths and ensures that good hygiene is maintained.

guide to recipe key		
	easy	Recipes are graded as follows: 1 pea = easy; 2 peas = very easy; 3 peas = extremely easy.
	serves 4	Recipes generally serve four people. Simply halve the ingredients to serve two, taking care not to mix imperial and metric measurements.
	10 minutes	Preparation time. Where marinating or soaking are involved, these times have been added on separately: e.g. 15 minutes + 30 minutes to marinate.
	10 minutes	Cooking time. Cooking times don't include the cooking of side dishes or accompaniments served with the main dishes.

gruyère fondue with pink champagne
page 30

thai firepot
page 46

vegetable tempura
page 62

mocha fondue
page 86

cheese
fondues

Cheese fondues make delicious, protein-rich meals, and wonderful conversation pieces for social occasions. You can ring the changes by experimenting with different cheeses. For example, many people know about the excellent melting qualities of Gruyère and Emmenthal cheeses, but Spanish manchego cheese (see page 22) or a goat's cheese such as Montrachet (see page 16) are excellent alternatives. These cheeses melt beautifully and will create a most memorable fondue with a distinctive taste that your guests will talk about long after the meal is finished.

swiss-style fondue with brandy

very easy		
serves 4		
10–15 minutes		
15–20 minutes		

ingredients

1 garlic clove, peeled and halved
425 ml/15 fl oz dry white wine
5 tbsp brandy
200 g/7 oz Gruyère cheese, grated
200 g/7 oz Emmenthal cheese, grated
200 g/7 oz Comté cheese, grated
100 g/3½ oz Parmesan cheese, grated
2 tbsp cornflour
pinch of freshly grated nutmeg
salt and pepper

DIPPERS
fresh crusty bread, cut into
 bite-sized pieces
small pieces of blanched asparagus

Rub the inside of a flameproof fondue pot with the garlic. Discard the garlic. Pour in the wine and 3 tablespoons of the brandy, then transfer to the hob and bring to a gentle simmer over a low heat.

Add a small handful of grated cheese and stir constantly until melted. Continue to add the cheese gradually, stirring constantly after each addition. Repeat until all the cheese has been added and stir until thoroughly melted and bubbling gently.

In a bowl, mix the cornflour with the remaining brandy. Stir the cornflour mixture into the fondue and continue to stir for 3–4 minutes, until thickened and bubbling. Stir in the nutmeg and season to taste with salt and pepper.

Using protective gloves, transfer the fondue pot to a lit tabletop burner. To serve, allow your guests to spear pieces of bread and asparagus on to fondue forks and dip them into the fondue.

french cheese fondue

very easy	
serves 4	
25 minutes, plus 20 minutes to cool	
1 hour 20–25 minutes	

ingredients

2 spring onions, trimmed and chopped
500 ml/18 fl oz dry white wine
350 g/12 oz Beaufort cheese, grated
350 g/12 oz Camembert cheese,
  rind removed, cut into small pieces
2 tbsp cornflour
pinch of cayenne pepper
salt and pepper

CRISPY POTATO SKINS
750 g/1 lb 10 oz medium potatoes
3 tbsp butter, melted
salt and pepper

DIPPERS
warm garlic bread or crusty French
  bread, cut into bite-sized pieces
blanched broccoli florets

To make the potato skins, preheat the oven to 200°C/400°F/ Gas Mark 6. Scrub the potatoes, pierce with a fork and bake for 50 minutes. Leave to cool. Cut each lengthways into 8 pieces. Scoop out most of the flesh, brush with butter and season. Arrange skin-side down on a baking sheet. Bake for 12–15 minutes, until crisp.

Put the spring onions into a flameproof fondue pot with all but 2 tablespoons of the wine. Transfer to the hob and bring to a simmer over a low heat. Add a small handful of cheese and stir until melted. Repeat until all the cheese has been added and is bubbling gently.

In a bowl, mix the cornflour with the remaining wine, stir into the fondue and continue to stir for 3–4 minutes, until thickened and bubbling. Stir in the cayenne and season to taste. Using protective gloves, transfer the fondue pot to a lit tabletop burner. To serve, allow your guests to spear potato skins, pieces of bread and broccoli florets on to fondue forks and dip them into the fondue.

brie & mushroom fondue

		ingredients	
	very easy	3 tbsp butter	350 g/12 oz Beaufort cheese, grated
		100 g/3½ oz button mushrooms, diced	2 tbsp cornflour
	serves 4	100 g/3½ oz chestnut	2 tbsp brandy
		mushrooms, diced	
		salt and pepper	DIPPERS
		1 tbsp chopped fresh parsley	warm garlic bread, cut into
	15 minutes	1 garlic clove, finely chopped	bite-sized pieces
		450 ml/16 fl oz dry white wine	baby new potatoes, steamed
		350 g/12 oz Brie, rind removed,	small whole mushrooms,
	25 minutes	cut into small pieces	lightly sautéed

Melt the butter in a frying pan over a medium heat. Add the diced mushrooms and cook, stirring, for 3–4 minutes, until tender. Season to taste with salt and pepper, then stir in the parsley. Remove from the heat and set aside. Put the garlic into a flameproof fondue pot and pour in the wine. Transfer to the hob and bring to a gentle simmer over a low heat. Add a small handful of cheese and stir constantly until melted. Continue to add the remaining cheese gradually, stirring constantly after each addition, then stir until thoroughly melted and bubbling gently. Stir in the reserved mushroom mixture in small batches, until incorporated.

In a bowl, mix the cornflour with the brandy. Stir this mixture into the fondue and continue to stir for 3–4 minutes, until thickened and bubbling. Taste and adjust the seasoning if necessary. Using protective gloves, transfer the fondue pot to a lit tabletop burner. To serve, allow your guests to spear pieces of garlic bread, potatoes and mushrooms on to fondue forks and dip them into the fondue.

pesto fondue

very easy	
serves 4	
15 minutes	
15–20 minutes	

ingredients

35 g/1¼ oz fresh basil, finely chopped
3 garlic cloves, finely chopped
300 g/10½ oz fontina cheese, chopped
250 g/9 oz ricotta cheese
50 g/1¾ oz Parmesan cheese, grated
2 tbsp lemon juice
375 ml/13 fl oz vegetable stock
1 tbsp cornflour
salt and pepper

DIPPERS
fresh Italian bread, such as ciabatta or
    focaccia, cut into bite-sized pieces
selection of lightly cooked vegetables,
    cut into bite-sized pieces

Put the basil and garlic into a large mixing bowl. Add all the cheeses and stir together well.

Put the lemon juice and all but 2 tablespoons of the stock into a large saucepan and bring to a gentle simmer over a low heat. Add a small spoonful of the cheese mixture and stir constantly until melted. Continue to add the cheese mixture gradually, stirring constantly after each addition. Repeat until all the cheese mixture has been added and stir until thoroughly melted and bubbling gently. Mix the cornflour with the remaining stock, then stir into the saucepan. Continue to stir for 3–4 minutes, until thickened and bubbling. Season to taste with salt and pepper.

Pour the mixture into a fondue pot and, using protective gloves, transfer to a lit tabletop burner. To serve, allow your guests to spear pieces of bread and vegetables on to fondue forks and dip them into the fondue.

montrachet & red pepper melt

		ingredients	
very easy		2 red peppers, cut into quarters and deseeded	DIPPERS whole green and black olives, stoned
serves 4		1 large garlic clove, finely chopped 250 ml/9 fl oz dry white wine 400 g/14 oz Gruyère cheese, grated	fresh crusty bread, cut into bite-sized pieces roasted courgettes, cut into
15 minutes		75 g/2¾ oz Montrachet cheese, or other goat's cheese if unavailable, cut into small pieces	bite-sized pieces red peppers, cut into bite-sized pieces
35 minutes		1 tbsp cornflour 1 tbsp chopped fresh parsley salt and pepper	

To skin the peppers, flatten them and arrange skin-side up on a grill rack lined with foil. Place under a hot grill for 10–15 minutes, until the skins are blackened. Transfer to a polythene bag, set aside for 15 minutes, then peel off the skins. Cut six of the pieces into bite-sized chunks and reserve for dippers. Finely dice the rest. Put the garlic and all but 2 tablespoons of the wine into a saucepan and bring to a gentle simmer over a low heat. Add a small handful of the Gruyère cheese and stir until melted. Add the remaining Gruyère gradually, stirring constantly after each addition. Add the diced red pepper, then stir in the Montrachet until melted.

In a bowl, mix the cornflour with the remaining wine, add to the saucepan and stir for 3–4 minutes, until thickened and bubbling. Stir in the parsley and season. Pour the mixture into a fondue pot and, using protective gloves, transfer to a lit tabletop burner. To serve, allow your guests to spear olives and pieces of bread, pepper and courgette on to fondue forks and dip them into the fondue.

fontina & wild mushroom
fondue with herbs

		ingredients	
very easy		2 tbsp butter	175 ml/6 fl oz dry white wine
		200 g/7 oz mixed wild mushrooms,	300 g/10½ oz fontina cheese, chopped
serves 4		such as shiitake, chanterelle and	300 g/10½ oz Emmenthal
		morel, roughly sliced	cheese, grated
		salt and pepper	1 tbsp cornflour
15–20 minutes		1 tbsp chopped fresh parsley	
		1 tbsp chopped fresh oregano	DIPPERS
		2 spring onions, trimmed and	fresh crusty bread, cut into
		finely chopped	bite-sized pieces
25 minutes		175 ml/6 fl oz vegetable stock	selection of lightly cooked vegetables,
		3 tbsp lemon juice	cut into bite-sized pieces

Melt the butter in a frying pan over a medium heat. Add the mushrooms and cook, stirring, for 3–4 minutes, until tender. Season to taste, then stir in the parsley and oregano. Remove from the heat and set aside. Put the spring onions into a flameproof fondue pot and pour in the stock, lemon juice and all but 2 tablespoons of the wine. Transfer to the hob and bring to a gentle simmer over a low heat. Add a small handful of cheese and stir until melted. Repeat until all the cheese has been added and stir until thoroughly melted and bubbling gently. Stir in the reserved mushroom mixture in small batches, until incorporated.

In a bowl, mix the cornflour with the remaining wine, then stir into the fondue. Continue to stir for 3–4 minutes, until thickened and bubbling. Taste and adjust the seasoning if necessary. Using protective gloves, transfer the fondue pot to a lit tabletop burner. To serve, allow your guests to spear pieces of bread and vegetables on to fondue forks and dip them into the fondue.

smoked cheddar & cider fondue

		ingredients	
very easy	2 tbsp lime juice	DIPPERS
	475 ml/17 fl oz dry cider	4 apples, cored and cut into bite-sized
serves 4	700 g/1 lb 9 oz smoked Cheddar	cubes, then brushed with lemon juice
	cheese, grated	fresh crusty bread, cut into
	2 tbsp cornflour	bite-sized cubes
10 minutes	pinch of ground mixed spice	canned pineapple chunks, drained
	salt and pepper	lean cooked ham, cut into
15 minutes		bite-sized cubes

Put the lime juice and all but 2 tablespoons of the cider into a large saucepan and bring to a gentle simmer over a low heat. Add a small handful of the cheese and stir until melted. Add the remaining cheese gradually, stirring constantly after each addition.

In a bowl, mix the cornflour with the remaining cider, then stir into the saucepan. Continue to stir for 3–4 minutes, until thickened and bubbling. Stir in the mixed spice and add salt and pepper to taste.

Pour the mixture into a fondue pot and, using protective gloves, transfer to a lit tabletop burner. To serve, allow your guests to spear pieces of apple, bread, pineapple and ham on to fondue forks and dip them into the fondue.

spanish manchego fondue
with olives

		ingredients	
very easy		1 garlic clove, peeled and halved	DIPPERS
serves 4		425 ml/15 fl oz Spanish dry white wine	fresh crusty bread, cut into
		finely grated rind of 1 lemon or lime	bite-sized pieces
10–15 minutes		700 g/1 lb 9 oz manchego cheese, grated	chorizo sausage, cut into bite-sized pieces and lightly fried in olive oil
15–20 minutes		2 tbsp cornflour salt and pepper	whole green and black olives, stoned

Rub the inside of a flameproof fondue pot with the garlic. Discard the garlic. Pour in the white wine and add the lemon rind, then transfer to the hob and bring to a gentle simmer over a low heat. Toss the cheese in the cornflour, then gradually stir the cheese into the heated liquid and stir constantly until melted. Continue to add the cheese gradually, stirring constantly, until all the cheese has melted and the liquid is bubbling gently. Stir until thick and creamy. Season to taste with salt and pepper.

Using protective gloves, transfer the fondue pot to a lit tabletop burner. To serve, allow your guests to spear bread, chorizo and olives on to fondue forks and dip them into the fondue.

three-cheese fondue
with caramelized onions

very easy	
serves 4	
15–20 minutes	
40 minutes	

ingredients

1 garlic clove, finely chopped
425 ml/15 fl oz dry white wine
250 g/9 oz mature Cheddar
    cheese, grated
250 g/9 oz Wensleydale
    cheese, crumbled
200 g/7 oz Somerset Brie or other Brie,
    rind removed, cut into small pieces
1 tbsp cornflour
2 tbsp brandy
salt and pepper

CARAMELIZED ONIONS
1 tbsp butter
1 tbsp olive oil
250 g/9 oz baby onions, peeled but
    left whole
1 tsp caster sugar
1 tsp balsamic vinegar

DIPPERS
warm garlic bread, cut into
    bite-sized pieces

First make the caramelized onions. Melt the butter and oil in a frying pan over a medium heat. Add the onions and cook, stirring, for 10 minutes. Sprinkle over the sugar and cook for 5 minutes, then stir in the vinegar. Cook for another 5 minutes, then remove from the heat and set aside. Put the garlic into a flameproof fondue pot and pour in the wine. Transfer to the hob and bring to a gentle simmer over a low heat. Add a small handful of cheese and stir until melted. Continue to add the cheese gradually, stirring constantly after each addition. Repeat until all the cheese has been added and stir until thoroughly melted and bubbling gently.

In a bowl, mix the cornflour with the brandy. Stir the cornflour mixture into the fondue and continue to stir for 3–4 minutes, until thickened and bubbling. Season to taste. Using protective gloves, transfer the fondue pot to a lit tabletop burner. To serve, allow your guests to spear the caramelized onions and pieces of garlic bread on to fondue forks and dip them into the fondue.

creamy blue cheese fondue

		ingredients	
very easy		1 garlic clove, peeled and halved	DIPPERS
		425 ml/15 fl oz dry white wine	fresh crusty bread, cut into
		5 tbsp brandy	bite-sized pieces
serves 4		350 g/12 oz Gruyère cheese, grated	bite-sized pieces of lightly cooked
		350 g/12 oz dolcelatte	vegetables wrapped in cooked ham
		cheese, crumbled	or strips of lightly cooked bacon
10–15 minutes		1 tbsp cornflour	
		2 tbsp single cream	
15–20 minutes		salt and pepper	

Rub the inside of a flameproof fondue pot with the garlic. Discard the garlic. Pour in the wine and 3 tablespoons of the brandy, then transfer to the hob and bring to a gentle simmer over a low heat. Add a small handful of cheese and stir constantly until melted. Continue to add the cheese gradually, stirring constantly after each addition, until all the cheese has been added. Stir until thoroughly melted and bubbling gently.

In a bowl, mix the cornflour with the remaining brandy. Stir the cornflour mixture into the fondue and continue to stir for 3–4 minutes, until thickened and bubbling. Stir in the cream and season to taste with salt and pepper.

Using protective gloves, transfer the fondue pot to a lit tabletop burner. To serve, allow your guests to spear pieces of bread and ham-wrapped vegetables on to fondue forks and dip them into the fondue.

greek cheese fondue

		ingredients	
very easy		1 large garlic clove, finely chopped	DIPPERS
		225 ml/8 fl oz Greek dry white wine	whole dark kalamata olives, stoned
		400 g/14 oz Emmenthal cheese, grated	warmed garlic pitta bread, cut into
serves 4		75 g/2¾ oz feta cheese, crumbled	bite-sized pieces
		1½ tbsp cornflour	skinned red peppers (see page 16),
		2 tbsp ouzo	cut into bite-sized pieces
15 minutes		1 tbsp chopped fresh coriander	
		salt and pepper	
20 minutes			

Put the garlic and all but 2 tablespoons of the wine into a large saucepan and bring to a gentle simmer over a low heat. Add a small handful of the Emmenthal cheese and stir until melted. Add the remaining Emmenthal gradually, stirring constantly after each addition. Add the feta cheese and stir until melted.

In a bowl, mix the cornflour with the ouzo, then stir into the saucepan. Continue to stir for 3–4 minutes, until thickened and bubbling. Stir in the coriander and add salt and pepper to taste.

Pour the mixture into a fondue pot and, using protective gloves, transfer to a lit tabletop burner. To serve, allow your guests to spear olives and pieces of pitta bread and red pepper on to fondue forks and dip them into the fondue.

gruyère fondue
with pink champagne

		ingredients

very easy	400 ml/14 fl oz pink champagne
	300 g/10½ oz Gruyère cheese, grated
	300 g/10½ oz Crottin de Chavignol
	  cheese, or other goat's cheese if
	  unavailable, cut into small pieces
	1 tbsp cornflour
	2 tbsp single cream
	salt and pepper
		DIPPERS
		fresh crusty bread, cut into
		  bite-sized pieces
		whole white seedless grapes

serves 4		
10 minutes		
15 minutes		

Pour the champagne into a flameproof fondue pot. Transfer to the hob and bring to a gentle simmer over a low heat. Add a small handful of Gruyère cheese and stir constantly until melted. Continue to add the Gruyère gradually, stirring constantly after each addition. Repeat until all the Gruyère has been added and stir until thoroughly melted and bubbling gently. Stir in the Crottin de Chavignol cheese until melted.

In a bowl, mix the cornflour with the cream. Stir the cornflour mixture into the fondue and continue to stir for 3–4 minutes, until thickened and bubbling. Season to taste with salt and pepper.

Using protective gloves, transfer the fondue pot to a lit tabletop burner. To serve, allow your guests to spear pieces of bread and grapes on to fondue forks and dip them into the fondue.

italian cheese fondue

		ingredients	
very easy		1 garlic clove, peeled and halved	DIPPERS
		450 ml/16 fl oz milk	fresh Italian bread, cut into
serves 4		3 tbsp brandy	bite-sized pieces
		300 g/10½ oz dolcelatte	salami, cut into bite-sized pieces
		cheese, crumbled	small pieces of apple, wrapped in
10–15 minutes		200 g/7 oz fontina cheese, chopped	Parma ham
		200 g/7 oz mozzarella cheese, chopped	morsels of roast chicken
		1 tbsp cornflour	
15 minutes		salt and pepper	

Rub the inside of a flameproof fondue pot with the garlic. Discard the garlic. Pour in the milk and 1 tablespoon of the brandy, then transfer to the hob and bring to a gentle simmer over a low heat.

Add a small handful of cheese and stir constantly until melted. Continue to add the cheese gradually, stirring constantly after each addition. Repeat until all the cheese has been added and stir until thoroughly melted and bubbling gently.

In a bowl, mix the cornflour with the remaining brandy. Stir the cornflour mixture into the fondue and continue to stir for 3–4 minutes, until thickened and bubbling. Season to taste with salt and pepper.

Using protective gloves, transfer the fondue pot to a lit tabletop burner. To serve, allow your guests to spear pieces of bread, salami, ham-wrapped apple, and chicken on to fondue forks and dip them into the fondue.

stock
fondues

Stock fondues are also known as 'Chinese firepots', and are a wonderfully healthy way to cook food. In this chapter there are recipes on offer to suit all tastes. The delicious stocks infuse each morsel of food with exciting flavours, and you will find the fragrant aromas of freshly cooked seafood, poultry and meat mouthwatering. Vegetarians will adore the nutritious Tofu & Vegetable Stockpot (see page 36), which is bursting with flavour, and for special occasions the Red Wine Fondue with Ravioli (see page 38) is unbeatable.

tofu & vegetable stockpot

	very easy	
	serves 4	
	20 minutes	
	1 hour 10 minutes	

ingredients

6 spring onions, trimmed and chopped
1 leek, trimmed and sliced
2 celery sticks
3 large carrots, peeled and chopped
1.2 litres/2 pints water
1 bouquet garni, made from fresh
    parsley, thyme and rosemary sprigs
    and a bay leaf
salt and pepper
1 garlic clove, peeled and halved
1 tbsp sherry

DIPPERS
200 g/7 oz firm tofu (drained weight),
    cut into bite-sized pieces
selection of vegetables, such as
    broccoli florets and button
    mushrooms, and red peppers,
    cut into bite-sized pieces

Put the spring onions, leek, celery, carrots and water into a large saucepan. Add the bouquet garni, season to taste with salt and pepper and bring to the boil. Reduce the heat and simmer for 1 hour. Remove from the heat and strain through a sieve into a large heatproof bowl. Discard the solids and reserve the liquid. Arrange the dippers on a serving platter or individual plates ready for cooking.

Rub the inside of a flameproof fondue pot with the garlic. Discard the garlic. Pour in the reserved liquid until the fondue pot is two-thirds full, then transfer to the hob and bring to boiling point over a medium heat. Stir in the sherry. Using protective gloves, transfer the fondue pot to a lit tabletop burner. To serve, allow your guests to spear the dippers on to fondue forks and dip them in the hot stock until cooked to their taste.

red wine fondue with ravioli

		ingredients	
easy		STOCK	4 eggs, beaten
		1 garlic clove, chopped	2 tbsp olive oil
		2 onions, chopped	1 onion, finely chopped
serves 4		2 celery sticks, chopped	4 tomatoes, peeled and finely chopped
		3 large carrots, peeled and chopped	100 g/3½ oz mushrooms, finely chopped
		1.2 litres/2 pints water	200 g/7 oz spinach leaves, blanched and
		1 bay leaf	finely chopped
50 minutes		3 fresh parsley sprigs	50 g/1¾ oz Parmesan cheese, grated
		salt and pepper	2 tbsp chopped fresh basil
		3 tbsp red wine	
			DIPPERS
1¼ hours		RAVIOLI	selection of blanched vegetables,
		450 g/1 lb durum wheat flour	cut into bite-sized pieces

To make the ravioli, sift the flour into a mound on a clean work surface and make a well. Add the eggs and half the oil and mix well. Knead for 10 minutes and set aside for 30 minutes. Halve the dough, then roll out thinly into 2 rectangles. Cover with a damp tea towel.

In a frying pan, cook the onion, tomatoes and mushrooms in the remaining oil over a medium heat for 10 minutes, or until the liquid has evaporated. Mix with the remaining ravioli ingredients. Place spoonfuls at intervals on one pasta rectangle. Cover with the other rectangle, cut into squares around the mounds and seal. Cover.

Bring all the stock ingredients to the boil in a pan, then reduce the heat and simmer for 1 hour. Strain into a heatproof bowl, discard the solids and pour into a flameproof fondue pot until two-thirds full, then bring to boiling point on the hob. Using protective gloves, transfer to a lit tabletop burner. To serve, spear the ravioli and dippers on to fondue forks and dip in the hot stock until cooked.

golden seafood fondue

		ingredients	
easy	1 kg/2 lb 4 oz live mussels	DIPPERS
	2 tbsp butter	200 g/7 oz raw shelled scallops
serves 4	2 garlic cloves, chopped	selection of blanched vegetables,
	4 spring onions, trimmed and chopped	cut into bite-sized pieces
	1.2 litres/2 pints dry white wine	
	125 ml/4 fl oz water	
15 minutes	1 bay leaf	
	250 ml/9 fl oz single cream	
	½ tsp ground saffron or turmeric	
25 minutes	salt and pepper	

Soak the mussels in lightly salted water for 10 minutes, then scrub the shells under cold running water. Pull off any beards. Discard any mussels with broken shells or that refuse to close when tapped.

Melt the butter in a large saucepan over a low heat. Add the garlic and spring onions and cook, stirring, for 3 minutes. Add the wine, water, bay leaf and mussels, bring to the boil and cook over a high heat for 4 minutes, until the mussels have opened. Discard any that remain closed. Strain the mussels, reserving the liquid, and shell them. Discard the bay leaf. Arrange the mussels with the dippers on serving plates. Pour the reserved liquid into a flameproof fondue pot until two-thirds full. Transfer to the hob and bring to boiling point over a medium heat. Stir in the cream and saffron and season to taste. Using protective gloves, transfer the fondue pot to a lit tabletop burner. To serve, allow your guests to spear the dippers on to fondue forks and dip them in the hot fondue for about 3–4 minutes, or until cooked to their taste.

prawn & scallop firepot

		ingredients	
	very easy	250 g/9 oz fine egg noodles	DIPPERS
		1.5 litres/2¾ pints fish stock or	300 g/10½ oz raw prawns,
	serves 4	vegetable stock	peeled and deveined
		2 garlic cloves, chopped	200 g/7 oz raw shelled scallops
		2 shallots, chopped	300 g/10½ oz sugar snap peas or
		1 tbsp grated fresh root ginger	mangetout, blanched
	20 minutes	1 tbsp grated fresh lemon grass	baby onions, peeled but left whole
		salt and pepper	
		1 tbsp rice wine or sherry	1 quantity Oriental Dipping Sauce
	20 minutes		(see page 78), to serve

Place the noodles in a heatproof bowl, cover with boiling water and leave to soak for 4 minutes, then drain and set aside. Pour the stock into a large saucepan and add the garlic, shallots, ginger, lemon grass and salt and pepper to taste. Bring to the boil, then reduce the heat and simmer for 15 minutes. Arrange the dippers on serving plates.

Stir the rice wine into the stock, then pour into a flameproof fondue pot (it should be no more than two-thirds full). Using protective gloves, transfer the fondue pot to a lit tabletop burner. To serve, allow your guests to spear the dippers on to fondue forks, dip them into the hot stock until cooked to their taste, then dip them in the dipping sauce. When all the dippers have been finished, add the noodles to the stock in the fondue pot and serve as a soup.

japanese seafood fondue

very easy	
serves 4	
30 minutes	
5 minutes	

ingredients

150 g/5½ oz cellophane noodles
350 g/12 oz firm-fleshed fish fillets,
 such as cod, haddock or monkfish,
 rinsed and cut into bite-sized pieces
1 litre/1¾ pints fish stock or
 vegetable stock
13-cm/5-inch piece kombu (dried kelp),
 cut into small pieces and rinsed in
 cold water
1 tbsp sake
6 tbsp soy sauce

DIPPERS
4 large peeled carrots, blanched and
 cut into bite-sized pieces
450 g/1 lb raw prawns,
 peeled and deveined
300 g/10½ oz sugar snap peas or
 mangetout, blanched

Place the noodles in a bowl, cover with cold water and leave to soak for 30 minutes, then drain and cut into 7.5-cm/3-inch lengths. Meanwhile, bring a large saucepan of water to the boil, add the fish pieces and cook briefly for 20 seconds. Drain, rinse under cold water and set aside.

Pour the stock into a large saucepan and add the kombu. Bring to the boil, then reduce the heat and simmer for 2 minutes. Pour in the sake. Arrange the fish on serving plates with the other dippers.

Pour the stock into a flameproof fondue pot (it should be no more than two-thirds full). Using protective gloves, transfer the fondue pot to a lit tabletop burner. To serve, allow your guests to spear the dippers on to fondue forks or place them on heatproof spoons, dip them into the hot stock until cooked to their taste, then dip them in the soy sauce. When all the dippers are finished, add the noodles to the stock in the fondue pot and serve as a soup.

thai firepot

		ingredients	

	very easy	250 g/9 oz rice noodles
		4 tbsp lemon juice
		3 tbsp vegetable oil
		1 fresh red chilli, deseeded and
		  finely chopped
		1 garlic clove, chopped
		3 tbsp chopped fresh coriander
		6 skinless, boneless chicken breasts,
		  cut into thin, bite-sized slices
		4 spring onions, trimmed and sliced
		1.2 litres/2 pints chicken stock or
		  vegetable stock
			1 tbsp grated fresh lemon grass
			½ tsp chilli powder
			salt and pepper
			
			DIPPERS
			selection of blanched vegetables,
			  cut into bite-sized pieces
			whole cooked peeled prawns
			
			1 quantity Oriental Dipping Sauce
			  (see page 78), to serve

	serves 4		
	1 ½ hours		
	30 minutes		

Place the noodles in a heatproof bowl, cover with boiling water and soak for 4 minutes. Drain and set aside. Pour the lemon juice into a large, shallow non-metallic dish. Pour in half of the oil, then add the chilli, garlic, coriander and chicken. Turn the chicken in the mixture, cover with clingfilm and refrigerate for 1¼ hours.

Heat the remaining oil in a saucepan over a medium heat. Add the spring onions and cook, stirring, for 3 minutes. Add the remaining ingredients. Bring to the boil, reduce the heat and simmer for 25 minutes. Drain the chicken and arrange on plates with the dippers.

Pour the stock into a flameproof fondue pot until two-thirds full. Using protective gloves, transfer to a lit tabletop burner. To serve, allow your guests to spear the dippers on to fondue forks, dip them into the hot stock until cooked to their taste (cook the chicken right through), then dip in the dipping sauce. When the dippers are finished, add the noodles to the stock and serve as soup.

sherried chicken fondue

		ingredients	
very easy		1 litre/1¾ pints chicken stock	DIPPERS
		100 ml/3½ fl oz white wine	750 g/1 lb 10 oz roast chicken breast,
serves 4		1 large garlic clove, chopped	cut into bite-sized pieces
		1 tsp sugar	2 red peppers, skinned (see page 16)
		4 tbsp sherry	and cut into bite-sized pieces
15 minutes			blanched broccoli and
			cauliflower florets
			peeled carrots, blanched and cut into
			bite-sized pieces
15 minutes			1 quantity Aïoli (see page 80), to serve

Pour the stock into a large saucepan and add the wine, garlic and sugar. Bring to the boil, then reduce the heat and simmer for 10 minutes. Arrange the dippers on serving plates.

Stir the sherry into the stock, then pour the stock into a flameproof fondue pot (it should be no more than two-thirds full). Using protective gloves, transfer the fondue pot to a lit tabletop burner. To serve, allow your guests to spear the dippers on to fondue forks, dip them into the hot stock until cooked to their taste, then dip them in the Aïoli.

fiery chicken fondue

		ingredients	
very easy	4 tbsp chilli oil	few drops of red food colouring
	1 tbsp lemon juice	(optional)
	2 garlic cloves, chopped	1 tbsp cornflour
serves 4	½ tsp paprika	
	½ tsp turmeric	DIPPERS
	6 skinless, boneless chicken	whole cherry tomatoes
	breasts, halved	whole black olives, stoned
1½ hours	salt and pepper	1 red pepper, skinned (see page 16)
	850 ml/1½ pints chicken stock	and cut into bite-sized pieces
	100 ml/3½ fl oz red wine	1 orange pepper, skinned (see page
	1 fresh red chilli, deseeded and	16) and cut into bite-sized pieces
20 minutes	finely chopped	
	1 tbsp tomato purée	freshly cooked rice, to serve

Place the oil, lemon juice and half of the garlic in a large, shallow non-metallic dish. Rub the chicken with the paprika and turmeric, then add to the oil mixture with salt and pepper to taste. Turn until coated. Cover with clingfilm and refrigerate for 1¼ hours.

Pour the stock into a large saucepan and pour in all but 2 tablespoons of the wine. Add the chilli, tomato purée, remaining garlic and the food colouring, if using. Bring to the boil, then reduce the heat and simmer for 10 minutes. Drain the chicken, cut into thin, bite-sized slices and arrange on serving plates with the dippers. In a bowl, mix the cornflour with the remaining wine, then stir into the saucepan. Continue to stir for 3–4 minutes, until thickened, then pour into a flameproof fondue pot until two-thirds full. Using protective gloves, transfer the fondue pot to a lit tabletop burner. To serve, allow your guests to spear the dippers on to fondue forks and dip them into the hot stock until cooked to their taste (cook the chicken right through). Serve with rice.

speared pork fondue
with noodles

		ingredients	
easy		4 tbsp lime juice	PEANUT SAUCE
		3 tbsp chilli oil	250 ml/9 fl oz coconut milk
		1 garlic clove, chopped	1 tsp red curry paste
serves 4		3 tbsp chopped fresh coriander	4 tbsp smooth peanut butter
		600 g/1 lb 5 oz pork fillet, cut into	1 tsp grated fresh root ginger
		thin slices	
		4 spring onions, trimmed and sliced	DIPPERS
1½ hours		1.2 litres/2 pints chicken stock or	200 g/7 oz firm tofu (drained weight),
		vegetable stock	cut into bite-sized pieces
		1 tbsp grated fresh lemon grass	selection of blanched vegetables,
30 minutes		½ tsp chilli powder	cut into bite-sized pieces
		salt and pepper	freshly cooked noodles, to serve

Pour the lime juice into a large, shallow non-metallic dish. Add half of the oil, the garlic, coriander and pork. Turn the pork in the mixture, cover with clingfilm and refrigerate for 1¼ hours.

Heat the remaining oil in a large saucepan over a medium heat. Add the spring onions and cook, stirring, for 3 minutes. Add the stock, lemon grass, chilli powder and salt and pepper to taste. Bring to the boil, then reduce the heat and simmer for 25 minutes. Meanwhile, to make the sauce, simmer the coconut milk in a separate saucepan for 15 minutes, then gradually stir in the remaining ingredients and simmer for 5 minutes. Drain the pork and thread on to wooden skewers. Pour the stock mixture into a flameproof fondue pot until two-thirds full. Using protective gloves, transfer to a lit tabletop burner. To serve, allow your guests to spear the dippers on to fondue forks and dip them into the hot stock with the pork skewers until cooked to their taste (cook the pork right through). Serve with noodles and the sauce.

shabu shabu

		ingredients	
very easy		1 litre/1¾ pints beef stock	DIPPERS
		13-cm/5-inch piece kombu (dried kelp),	800 g/1 lb 12 oz beef sirloin, cut into
serves 4		cut into small pieces and rinsed in	thin, bite-sized strips
		cold water	200 g/7 oz firm tofu (drained weight),
		5 tbsp soy sauce	cut into bite-sized pieces
10–15		6 tbsp lime juice	8 spring onions, trimmed and cut into
minutes		400 g/14 oz precooked udon noodles,	bite-sized pieces
		or rice noodles if unavailable	
5–10			
minutes			

Pour the stock into a large saucepan and add the kombu. Bring to the boil, then reduce the heat and simmer for 5 minutes. Meanwhile, mix the soy sauce and lime juice in a small heatproof bowl, then stir in 1 tablespoon of stock from the saucepan and set aside. Arrange the dippers on serving plates.

Pour the stock and kombu into a flameproof fondue pot (it should be no more than two-thirds full). Using protective gloves, transfer the fondue pot to a lit tabletop burner. To serve, allow your guests to spear the dippers on to fondue forks or place them on heatproof spoons, dip them into the hot stock until cooked to their taste (cook the beef right through), then dip them in the soy sauce mixture. When all the dippers have been finished, add the noodles to the stock in the fondue pot and serve as a soup.

sizzlers
& dipping
sauces

Oil fondues offer an exciting and dramatic way to present food to your guests, and will ensure that any dinner party gets off to a sizzling start. Remember to use a sturdy metal fondue pot and place it securely, with its burner, on a heatproof surface where it cannot be knocked over. Pat dry with kitchen paper any marinated foods before immersing them in the hot oil, otherwise they may sputter and splash your guests. Following simple rules of safety like these will ensure that your meal goes without a hitch and is savoured by everyone.

crispy spring rolls

		ingredients	
easy		2 tbsp chilli oil	2 tbsp butter, melted
		4 spring onions, trimmed and finely chopped	1 egg white, slightly beaten
serves 4		1 red pepper, deseeded and finely sliced into 5-cm/2-inch lengths	1 litre/1¾ pints groundnut oil
		1 carrot, peeled and finely sliced into 5-cm/2-inch lengths	DIPPERS selection of vegetables, cut into bite-sized pieces
20 minutes		85 g/3 oz beansprouts	
		1 tbsp lemon juice	TO SERVE
		1 tsp soy sauce	1 quantity Oriental Dipping Sauce (see page 78)
10 minutes		salt and pepper	freshly cooked rice
		8 sheets filo pastry, halved	

Heat the chilli oil in a wok or large frying pan. Add the spring onions, red pepper and carrot and stir-fry for 2 minutes. Add the beansprouts, lemon juice and soy sauce and stir-fry for 1 minute, then add salt and pepper to taste and remove from the heat.

Spread out the pastry on a clean work surface and brush with melted butter. Spoon a little of the vegetable mixture on to one short end of each sheet of pastry, fold in the long sides and roll up to enclose the filling. Brush the edges with egg white to seal.

Pour the groundnut oil into a metal fondue pot (it should be no more than one-third full). Heat on the hob to 190°C/375°F, or until a cube of bread browns in 30 seconds. Using protective gloves, transfer the fondue pot to a lit tabletop burner. To serve, allow your guests to spear the spring rolls and dippers on to fondue forks and dip into the hot oil until cooked to taste (the spring rolls will need 2–3 minutes). Drain off the excess oil. Serve with the dipping sauce and rice.

golden cheese melts

	easy	
	serves 4	
	15 minutes	
	10 minutes	

ingredients

250 g/9 oz plain flour
¼ tsp cayenne pepper
400 g/14 oz Edam cheese,
   rind removed and cut into
   bite-sized cubes
1 tsp baking powder
1 tsp salt
2 large eggs
125 ml/4 fl oz milk
1 litre/1¾ pints groundnut oil

DIPPERS
whole button mushrooms
whole cherry tomatoes
blanched broccoli florets

fresh mixed salad, to serve

Sift 150 g/5½ oz of the flour with the cayenne pepper into a large bowl. Add the cheese cubes and turn until coated. Shake off the excess flour, then arrange the cheese on a serving platter. Put the remaining flour into a large bowl with the baking powder and salt, then gradually beat in the eggs, milk and 1 tablespoon of the oil. Beat until the batter is smooth, then pour it into a serving bowl.

Pour the remaining oil into a metal fondue pot (it should be no more than one-third full), then heat on the hob to 190°C/375°F, or until a cube of bread browns in 30 seconds. Using protective gloves, carefully transfer the fondue pot to a lit tabletop burner. To serve, allow your guests to spear the cheese cubes on to fondue forks, dip in the batter and let the excess run off, then cook in the hot oil for 1 minute, or until golden and crisp. Cook the other dippers in the same way, or leave them without batter and cook to your taste. Drain off the excess oil and serve with a mixed salad.

vegetable tempura

easy	
serves 4	
15 minutes	
15–20 minutes	

ingredients

6 tbsp cornflour
6 tbsp soy sauce
6 tbsp lemon juice
1 litre/1¾ pints groundnut oil
1 egg
225 ml/8 fl oz ice-cold water
140 g/5 oz plain flour

DIPPERS
broccoli florets
button mushrooms
aubergine, cut into bite-sized pieces
baby corn cobs, halved
mangetout
cherry tomatoes

freshly cooked noodles, to serve

Put the cornflour into a bowl and turn all the vegetable dippers in it until coated. Shake off the excess cornflour, then arrange them on a serving platter. In a serving bowl, make a dipping sauce by mixing together the soy sauce and lemon juice, then set aside.

Pour the oil into a metal fondue pot (it should be no more than one-third full), then heat on the hob to 190°C/375°F, or until a cube of bread browns in 30 seconds. Using protective gloves, carefully transfer the fondue pot to a lit tabletop burner.

In a separate serving bowl, beat the egg and water together, then stir in the flour briefly. Do not overbeat: the batter should be lumpy. To serve, allow your guests to spear the dippers on to fondue forks, dip them in the batter and let the excess run off, then cook in the hot oil for 2–3 minutes, or until cooked to their taste. Drain off the excess oil, then serve with the dipping sauce and noodles.

spiced crab balls

easy	
serves 4	
1¼ hours	
15–20 minutes	

ingredients

450 g/1 lb frozen crabmeat, thawed
2 tbsp freshly grated lime rind
1 fresh red chilli, deseeded and
   finely chopped
1 tbsp finely chopped spring onion
1 tbsp grated fresh root ginger
1 tbsp grated fresh coconut
2 egg yolks
4 tsp cornflour
4 tbsp thick natural yogurt
2 tbsp sherry

salt and pepper
1 litre/1¾ pints groundnut oil

DIPPERS
200 g/7 oz firm tofu (drained weight),
   cut into bite-sized pieces
selection of vegetables, cut into
   bite-sized pieces

TO SERVE
1 quantity Oriental Dipping Sauce
   (see page 78)
freshly cooked rice

Put the crabmeat, lime rind, chilli, spring onion, ginger, coconut and egg yolk into a bowl and mix together well. Mix the cornflour with the yogurt and sherry in a small saucepan, place over a low heat and stir until thickened. Remove from the heat, mix into the bowl with the crabmeat mixture and season to taste with salt and pepper. Pull off pieces of the mixture and shape into 2.5-cm/1-inch balls. Cover with clingfilm and chill for at least 1 hour. Arrange the other dippers on serving plates.

Pour the oil into a metal fondue pot (it should be no more than one-third full), then heat on the hob to 190°C/375°F, or until a cube of bread browns in 30 seconds. Using protective gloves, carefully transfer the fondue pot to a lit tabletop burner. To serve, allow your guests to spear the dippers on to fondue forks (place the crab balls on spoons if not firm enough to spear), then cook in the hot oil for about 2–3 minutes, or until cooked to their taste. Drain off the excess oil, then serve with the dipping sauce and rice.

tuna & red chilli sizzlers

		ingredients	
easy	2 tbsp grated pecorino cheese	RED CHILLI DIPPING SAUCE
	2 eggs	125 ml/4 fl oz natural yogurt
serves 4	5 tbsp plain flour	4 tbsp mayonnaise
	175 g/6 oz canned tuna, flaked	1 fresh red chilli, deseeded and
	1 tbsp grated fresh root ginger	finely chopped
	1 tbsp grated lemon rind	1 tbsp lime juice
20 minutes	100 g/3½ oz sweetcorn kernels	
	½ tsp finely chopped fresh red chilli	DIPPERS
	1 litre/1¾ pints groundnut oil	selection of vegetables, cut into
15–20 minutes		bite-sized pieces
	fresh mixed salad, to serve	whole cooked peeled prawns

Put the cheese, eggs and flour into a large bowl and beat together. Add the tuna, ginger, lemon rind, sweetcorn and the ½ teaspoon of chopped red chilli and stir together well. Meanwhile, to make the sauce, put all the ingredients into a non-metallic serving bowl, mix together and set aside. Arrange the dippers on serving plates.

Pour the oil into a metal fondue pot (it should be no more than one-third full), then heat on the hob to 190°C/375°F, or until a cube of bread browns in 30 seconds. Using protective gloves, carefully transfer the fondue pot to a lit tabletop burner. To serve, allow your guests to spear the dippers on to fondue forks and cook them with dessertspoonfuls of the tuna mixture (using heatproof spoons) in the hot oil for about 3 minutes, or until cooked to their taste. Drain off the excess oil, then serve with the dipping sauce and a mixed salad.

skewered chicken
with mustard dip

		ingredients
easy	½ tsp turmeric 6 skinless, boneless chicken breasts salt and pepper 1 litre/1¾ pints groundnut oil	MUSTARD DIP 4 tbsp soured cream 4 tbsp mayonnaise 2 tbsp wholegrain mustard 1 tsp honey
serves 4	DIPPERS	1 spring onion, trimmed and finely chopped
15 minutes	4 rashers unsmoked streaky bacon cherry tomatoes whole baby onions, peeled	pinch of paprika
15–20 minutes	button mushrooms	sautéed new potatoes and a fresh mixed salad, to serve

Rub the turmeric over the chicken, then season and cut into strips. Stretch the bacon until doubled in length and cut into thin strips lengthways. Roll up the slices of chicken and bacon and thread them on to wooden skewers with the other dippers, leaving plenty of space at either end. Skewer the tomatoes separately, as they will need less time to cook. Mix the ingredients for the dip in a bowl.

Pour the oil into a metal fondue pot (it should be no more than one-third full), then heat on the hob to 190°C/375°F, or until a cube of bread browns in 30 seconds. Using protective gloves, carefully transfer the fondue pot to a lit tabletop burner.

Allow guests to dip the skewers into the fondue, and cook in the hot oil for 2–3 minutes, or until cooked to taste (cook the chicken and bacon right through). Drain off the excess oil, then serve with potatoes, salad and the dip.

oriental beef fondue

easy	
serves 4	
1½ hours	
15 minutes	

ingredients

6 tbsp soy sauce
5 tbsp dry sherry
1 garlic clove, chopped
1 tbsp grated fresh root ginger
1 tsp sugar
800 g/1 lb 12 oz fillet steak, cut into
 thin, bite-sized strips
1 litre/1¾ pints groundnut oil

DIPPERS
selection of vegetables, cut into
 bite-sized pieces

TO SERVE
1 quantity Oriental Dipping Sauce
 (see page 78)
freshly cooked noodles

Put the soy sauce, sherry, garlic, ginger and sugar into a large, shallow dish and mix together. Add the strips of steak and turn them in the mixture. Cover with clingfilm and refrigerate for 1¼ hours.

Drain the steak, pat dry with kitchen paper and thread on to wooden skewers, leaving plenty of space at either end. Arrange the skewers on serving plates with the other dippers.

Pour the oil into a metal fondue pot (it should be no more than one-third full), then heat on the hob to 190°C/375°F, or until a cube of bread browns in 30 seconds. Using protective gloves, carefully transfer the fondue pot to a lit tabletop burner.

To serve, allow your guests to spear the dippers on to fondue forks and dip them into the hot oil with the beef skewers until cooked to their taste (cook the beef right through). Drain off the excess oil, then serve with the dipping sauce and noodles.

fondue bourguignonne
with rich tomato sauce

		ingredients	
easy		800 g/1 lb 12 oz fillet steak, cut into 2-cm/¾-inch cubes	2 tbsp red wine
		1 litre/1¾ pints groundnut oil	1 tbsp chopped fresh parsley
serves 4		salt and pepper	1 tbsp chopped fresh oregano
		RICH TOMATO SAUCE	DIPPERS
15–20 minutes		1 tbsp olive oil	baby onions, peeled but left whole
		1 garlic clove, finely chopped	button mushrooms
		1 onion, finely chopped	cherry tomatoes
45–50 minutes		400 g/14 oz canned chopped tomatoes	crusty French bread, to serve
		1 tbsp tomato purée	

First make the tomato sauce. Heat the olive oil in a small saucepan over a medium heat, add the garlic and onion and cook, stirring, for 3 minutes, until softened. Stir in the tomatoes, tomato purée and wine. Bring to the boil, then reduce the heat and simmer gently, stirring occasionally, for about 25 minutes. Remove from the heat, stir in the parsley and oregano and set aside. Arrange the cubes of steak and the other dippers on serving plates.

Pour the groundnut oil into a metal fondue pot (it should be no more than one-third full), then heat on the hob to 190°C/375°F, or until a cube of bread browns in 30 seconds. Using protective gloves, carefully transfer the fondue pot to a lit tabletop burner.

To serve, allow your guests to spear the steak cubes and dippers on to fondue forks and dip them into the hot oil until cooked (cook the steak right through). Drain off the excess oil, season, then serve with bread and the sauce (you can serve the sauce hot or cold).

spicy pork satay

		ingredients

easy	2 tbsp lemon juice
	3 tbsp vegetable oil
	1 garlic clove, chopped
	2 tbsp chopped fresh coriander
	1 tbsp grated fresh lemon grass
	1 fresh red chilli, deseeded and
	  finely chopped
	800 g/1 lb 12 oz pork fillet, cut into
	  thin slices
	1 litre/1¾ pints groundnut oil
	salt and pepper
	
	freshly cooked rice, to serve
		SATAY SAUCE
		1 tsp chilli oil
		1 garlic clove, crushed
		1 spring onion, trimmed and
		  finely chopped
		1 fresh red chilli, deseeded and
		  finely chopped
		1 tsp Thai red curry paste
		5 tbsp crunchy peanut butter
		250 ml/9 fl oz coconut milk
		
		DIPPERS
		selection of fresh vegetables, cut into
		  bite-sized pieces

serves 4		
1½ hours		
20 minutes		

Pour the lemon juice into a large, shallow non-metallic dish. Add the vegetable oil, garlic, coriander, lemon grass, chilli and pork. Turn the pork in the mixture, cover with clingfilm and refrigerate for 1¼ hours. Drain the pork, pat dry with kitchen paper and arrange on a serving platter with the other dippers.

For the sauce, heat the chilli oil in a saucepan, add the garlic and spring onion and cook, stirring, for 3 minutes. Stir in the remaining ingredients, bring to the boil, then reduce the heat to a simmer.

Pour the groundnut oil into a metal fondue pot (it should be no more than one-third full), then heat on the hob to 190°C/375°F, or until a cube of bread browns in 30 seconds. Using protective gloves, carefully transfer the fondue pot to a lit tabletop burner. To serve, allow your guests to spear the pork and dippers on to fondue forks and dip into the hot oil until cooked (cook the pork right through). Drain off the excess oil, season, then serve with rice and the sauce.

crispy pork sausages

		### ingredients	
easy		450 g/1 lb pork sausagemeat	DIPPERS
		1 small onion, grated	button mushrooms
serves 4		6 tbsp grated Cheddar cheese	aubergine, cut into bite-sized pieces
		1 tbsp tomato purée	
		25 g/1 oz fresh breadcrumbs	TO SERVE
25 minutes		1 tsp turmeric	1 quantity Mustard Dip (see page 68)
		½ tsp paprika	1 quantity Crispy Potato Skins
		salt and pepper	(see page 10)
		2 eggs, beaten	warm crusty bread
15–20 minutes		100 g/3½ oz dried breadcrumbs	
		1 litre/1¾ pints groundnut oil	

Put the sausagemeat into a large bowl with the onion, cheese, tomato purée, fresh breadcrumbs, turmeric and paprika, and season to taste. Mix together well and, using your hands, shape into small sausages about 5 cm/2 inches long. Turn them in the beaten egg, then coat them in dried breadcrumbs. Arrange the sausages on a serving platter with the other dippers.

Pour the oil into a metal fondue pot (it should be no more than one-third full), then heat on the hob to 190°C/375°F, or until a cube of bread browns in 30 seconds. Using protective gloves, carefully transfer the fondue pot to a lit tabletop burner.

To serve, allow your guests to spear the pork sausages and other dippers on to fondue forks and dip into the hot oil until cooked to their taste (cook the sausages right through – they will need at least 3–4 minutes). Drain off the excess oil, then serve with the dip, bread and Crispy Potato Skins.

oriental dipping sauce

extremely easy	
serves 4	
35–40 minutes	
7–8 minutes	

ingredients

100 ml/3½ fl oz rice wine vinegar
finely grated rind and juice of 1 lime
2 tbsp soy sauce
250 g/9 oz granulated sugar
1 tbsp grated fresh root ginger
1 tbsp grated fresh lemon grass

2 garlic cloves, crushed
1 fresh red chilli, deseeded and
  finely chopped
2 tbsp sherry
1 tbsp chopped fresh coriander

Put the vinegar, lime rind and juice, soy sauce and sugar into a small saucepan and place over a medium heat. Stir in the ginger, lemon grass, garlic and chilli and bring to the boil, stirring constantly. Reduce the heat and simmer, stirring, for 5 minutes.

Stir in the sherry and coriander, heat through for another minute, then remove from the heat and strain through a sieve into a heatproof non-metallic serving bowl.

Leave to cool to room temperature, then serve.

aïoli

		ingredients	
extremely easy		3 large garlic cloves, finely chopped	1 tbsp Dijon mustard
		2 egg yolks	1 tbsp chopped fresh tarragon
serves 4		225 ml/8 fl oz extra virgin olive oil	salt and pepper
		1 tbsp lemon juice	sprig of tarragon, to decorate
		1 tbsp lime juice	
15 minutes			
—			

Ensure that the ingredients are all at room temperature. Put the garlic and the egg yolks into a food processor and process until well blended. With the motor running, pour in the oil teaspoon-by-teaspoon through the feeder tube until it starts to thicken, then pour in the remaining oil in a thin stream until a thick mayonnaise forms.

Add the lemon and lime juices, along with the mustard and tarragon, and season to taste with salt and pepper. Blend until smooth, then transfer to a non-metallic bowl. Decorate with a sprig of tarragon.

Cover with clingfilm and refrigerate until needed.

dessert fondues

There is no better way to round off a meal than with a luxuriously indulgent sweet fondue. Chocolate lovers will adore the Deep Chocolate Fondue (see page 84) and the Mocha Fondue (see page 86), and Butterscotch Fondue with Popcorn (see page 92) will prove irresistible to children and adults alike. For those of you who would like to add an extra sizzle to your meal's finale, the Chocolate Wontons with Maple Sauce (see page 94) will capture everyone's imagination and have the whole household clamouring for more.

deep chocolate fondue

very easy	
serves 4	
5–10 minutes	
10–15 minutes	

ingredients

250 g/9 oz plain chocolate
(must contain at least 50 per cent
cocoa solids)
100 ml/3½ fl oz double cream
2 tbsp brandy

DIPPERS
plain sponge cake, cut into
bite-sized pieces
small pink and white marshmallows
small firm whole fresh fruits, such as
blackcurrants, blueberries, cherries
and strawberries
whole no-soak dried apricots
crystallised citrus peel, cut decoratively
into strips or bite-sized pieces

Arrange the dippers decoratively on a serving platter or individual serving plates and set aside.

Break or chop the chocolate into small pieces and place in the top of a double boiler or in a heatproof bowl set over a saucepan of simmering water. Pour in the cream and stir until melted and smooth. Stir in the brandy, then carefully pour the mixture into a warmed fondue pot.

Using protective gloves, transfer the fondue pot to a lit tabletop burner. To serve, allow your guests to spear the dippers on to fondue forks and dip them into the fondue.

mocha fondue

		ingredients	
very easy		250 g/9 oz plain chocolate (must contain at least 50 per cent cocoa solids)	DIPPERS sweet biscuits, such as amaretti plain or coffee-flavoured marbled
serves 4		100 ml/3½ fl oz double cream 1 tbsp instant coffee powder 3 tbsp coffee-flavoured liqueur, such as Kahlúa	cake or sponge cake, cut into bite-sized pieces whole seedless grapes sliced firm peaches or nectarines
5–10 minutes			
10–15 minutes			

Arrange the dippers decoratively on a serving platter or individual serving plates and set aside.

Break or chop the chocolate into small pieces and place in the top of a double boiler or in a heatproof bowl set over a saucepan of simmering water. Add the cream and coffee powder and stir until melted and smooth. Stir in the liqueur, then carefully pour the mixture into a warmed fondue pot.

Using protective gloves, transfer the fondue pot to a lit tabletop burner. To serve, allow your guests to spear the dippers on to fondue forks and dip them into the fondue.

creamy caramel fondue

easy	
serves 4	
5–10 minutes	
10 minutes	

ingredients

125 g/4½ oz caster sugar
4 tbsp water
350 ml/12 fl oz double cream, gently warmed
3 tbsp rum

DIPPERS
plain sponge cake, cut into bite-sized pieces
firm ripe bananas, cut into bite-sized pieces
sliced apples

Arrange the dippers decoratively on a serving platter or individual serving plates and set aside.

Put the sugar and water into a heavy-based saucepan, place over a low heat and stir until the sugar has dissolved. Bring to the boil, then leave to bubble for 3–4 minutes. Stir in the warmed cream and continue to stir for 4–5 minutes, until smooth and well combined. Stir in the rum and cook for another minute. Remove from the heat and carefully pour the mixture into a warmed fondue pot.

Using protective gloves, transfer the fondue pot to a lit tabletop burner. To serve, allow your guests to spear the dippers on to fondue forks and dip them into the fondue.

rich toffee fondue

		ingredients	
	easy	125 g/4½ oz butter	DIPPERS
		400 g/14 oz brown sugar	sweet biscuits
		225 ml/8 fl oz golden syrup	firm ripe bananas, cut into
	serves 4	2 tbsp maple syrup	bite-sized pieces
		2 tbsp water	sliced apples
		400 ml/14 fl oz canned condensed milk	bite-sized pieces of chocolate
	10 minutes	1 tsp vanilla extract	miniature fairy cakes
		½ tsp ground cinnamon	shelled nuts, such as pecan or Brazil
		1 tbsp rum	nuts, and walnut halves
	10 minutes		

Arrange the dippers decoratively on a serving platter or individual serving plates and set aside.

Put the butter into a heatproof bowl set over a saucepan of simmering water and melt gently. Add the sugar, golden syrup, maple syrup, water, condensed milk, vanilla extract and cinnamon. Stir until thickened and smooth, then stir in the rum and cook for another minute. Remove from the heat and carefully pour the mixture into a warmed fondue pot.

Using protective gloves, transfer the fondue pot to a lit tabletop burner. To serve, allow your guests to spear the dippers on to fondue forks and dip them into the fondue.

butterscotch fondue
with popcorn

		ingredients		
easy	350 g/12 oz brown sugar	DIPPERS		
	125 ml/4 fl oz water	popcorn		
serves 4	1 tbsp rum	firm ripe bananas, cut into		
	6 tbsp unsalted butter	bite-sized pieces		
	125 ml/4 fl oz double cream,	sliced apples		
5–10 minutes	gently warmed			
	85 g/3 oz peanuts, chopped			
10–15 minutes				

Arrange the dippers decoratively on a serving platter or individual serving plates and set aside.

Put the sugar and water into a heavy-based saucepan, place over a medium heat and stir until the sugar has dissolved. Bring to the boil, then leave to bubble for 6–7 minutes. Stir in the rum and cook for another minute.

Using protective gloves, remove from the heat and carefully stir in the butter until melted. Gradually stir in the cream until the mixture is smooth. Finally, stir in the nuts.

Carefully pour the mixture into a warmed fondue pot, then transfer to a lit tabletop burner. To serve, allow your guests to spear the dippers on to fondue forks and dip them into the fondue.

chocolate wontons
with maple sauce

		ingredients	
easy	16 wonton wrappers	MAPLE SAUCE	
	350 g/12 oz plain chocolate, chopped	175 ml/6 fl oz maple syrup	
serves 4	1 tbsp cornflour	4 tbsp butter	
	3 tbsp cold water	½ tsp ground mixed spice	
	1 litre/1¾ pints groundnut oil		
15 minutes		vanilla ice cream, to serve	
15 minutes			

Spread out the wonton wrappers on a clean work surface, then spoon a little chopped chocolate into the centre of each wrapper. In a small bowl, mix together the cornflour and water until smooth. Brush the edges of the wrappers with the cornflour mixture, then wrap in any preferred shape, such as triangles, squares or bundles, and seal the edges. Arrange the wontons on a serving platter. To make the maple sauce, put all the ingredients into a saucepan and stir over a medium heat. Bring to the boil, then reduce the heat and simmer for 3 minutes.

Meanwhile, pour the oil into a metal fondue pot (it should be no more than one-third full). Heat on the hob to 190°C/375°F, or until a cube of bread browns in 30 seconds. Using protective gloves, transfer the fondue pot to a lit tabletop burner. To serve, allow your guests to place the wontons on metal spoons and dip them into the hot oil until cooked (they will need about 2–3 minutes). Drain off the excess oil. Serve with vanilla ice cream and the sauce.

index